Basic

LEARNING GUIDES©

HOW TO WRITE A

Resume & Cover Letter

Trilobyte Press

Basic Concepts
LEARNING GUIDES©

How to Write a Resume & Cover Letter

First published in 1993 by
TRILOBYTE PRESS
1486 Willowdown Road
Oakville, ON
Canada, L6L 1X3

Printed by Pocket Press

Canadian Cataloguing in Publication Data

Main entry under title:

How to write a resume & cover letter

(Basic concepts learning guides)

Based on the video kit Resumes that work by Evelyn K. Paley.

ISBN 1-895482-17-8

1. Resumes (Employment) I. Series.

HF5383.H68 1993 650.14 C93-094675-8

Basic Concepts
LEARNING GUIDES©

HOW TO WRITE A RESUME & COVER LETTER

TABLE OF CONTENTS

Chapter One

INTRODUCTION

LOOKING FOR A JOB CAN BE INTIMIDATING

Looking for a job can be very intimidating when you are new to the game. You should take some comfort in knowing that you are not alone. Most students are in the same boat. Few students or recent graduates have much work experience. What little they do have is often limited to the basic service-type of work training. While this may not sound like much, don't under-rate the value of any such experience in your quest for other employment.

Flipping burgers and selling jeans or other related work has given you some useful knowledge. For example, you've probably learned how to relate to other co-workers and to deal effectively with customers. You have likely learned to cope with the approaches of different supervisors or bosses. If you put this in the right way in your resume and reflect it properly in your cover letter, you can greatly improve your chances of finding a job.

When you have little job experience, it is very important to write the best resume and cover letter that you can. You will be selling yourself more on your potential than on directly related work experience. In preparing your resume it will be necessary to take a critical look at yourself. You will also have to evaluate yourself in terms of the jobs you are hoping to get and what the employer is looking for.

This booklet is designed to help you do these things. It will teach you how to prepare a personalized resume that best reflects your abilities, as they relate to the positions for which you will be applying. In this booklet we'll focus upon the chronological resume and a modified version of it as a basic starting point. These are the most common styles used by the beginning job seeker. Later you'll learn how to write an effective cover letter to get the attention of potential employers.

Let's begin with the resume by looking at its structure and some examples. Then we'll go through the process step-by-step. Later we'll do the same for writing a cover letter.

THE PURPOSE OF THE RESUME

The resume is a quick way of telling potential employers about you as an individual and your abilities as a future employee. It is a short synopsis of your educational and employment history, interests, skills and accomplishments. It is designed to convince an employer to interview you for potential job opportunities.

IMPORTANT POINTS ABOUT YOUR RESUME

The basic resume should:

- be 1 to 2 pages long
- be concise
- provide an overview of what you have done
- give insight into your abilities
- be a positive reflection of you as a person
- be results/action oriented

Your resume should reflect you as a person, especially your:

- communication skills
- ability to take the initiative
- ability to be responsible
- positive attitude

Chapter Two

THE FIRST DRAFT

THE FIRST STEP: LIST YOUR ACCOMPLISHMENTS

As with anything, you should start simply. One of the first things you will do in preparing your resume is to list the things you have done that you feel particularly good about. Think about your personal strengths in your work, education and areas of interest. For example, mention if you've had an evaluation or more formal performance past employer which congratulated you on some aspect of your work. In that review, you might have been told that you were quick to learn. In your job, you might have suggested an idea that your employer adopted with positive results. In terms of your schoolwork, you may have a high average. This should be stated.

At first, you may think there's nothing to put down. It should quickly become clear that everyone has achievements that they should feel positive about. If you have difficulty assessing yourself, ask a friend or counselor for help. This exercise will put you in a positive state of mind. You can then incorporate these accomplishments throughout the appropriate sections of your resume.

THE SECOND STEP: REVIEW YOUR EDUCATION, SPECIAL SKILLS, WORK HISTORY & ACCOMPLISHMENTS

Continue on by looking at the list below and filling in the worksheet that is included at the end of this chapter. Make a copy of the worksheet rather than writing in this booklet. If possible, use the photocopier to enlarge the worksheet so it is easier to work with. Fill it in as you work through this chapter. Then when you look at the examples and hints that follow, you probably will think of other things to add. Like you, your resume should grow with time and experience.

EDUCATION
(Diplomas/Certificates, etc.)

In this section list all relevant aspects of your education. Don't forget courses or training sessions that have been taken outside of your regular schooling.

Make sure you include:

- program of study (e.g., Secondary School Diploma, B.A.)
- area of focus or specialization, if applicable (e.g., English, Mathematics, Chemistry, etc.)
- specific dates of courses, graduation, etc.
- names of institutions where courses were taken or diploma was obtained
- overall marks, if they were good, plus single out any excellent grades where it particularly applies to the work you're seeking
- emphasize any relevant courses or projects if they relate to your chosen area of work

SPECIAL SKILLS

Here, you should include any special skills that you have. Employers are looking for practical abilities that they can immediately put to work. Be as clear as possible as to what those skills are.

Areas where you might have special skills are:

- Computers
- Languages
- Business related
- Lab/Research related

WORK HISTORY

All previous work experience should be listed.

Don't forget to include the following information:

- Dates, Position Title, Organization Name, Location (city, town only)
- Duties that you performed
- Emphasize your achievements and accomplishments
- Stress any increases in responsibility and any promotions
- Challenges that you faced: pressure, deadlines, long hours, etc.
- Emphasize skills you have developed

INTERESTS

An employer is not only looking for an individual with the proper skills and ability to do the job, but also a person who can fit into their special workplace environment.

In some jobs, interpersonal skills are very important. In others, being able to work alone and initiate projects will be essential. These attributes are often demonstrated by your personal interests.

Don't forget to:

- Tell how you spend your spare time
- List your hobbies: clubs, offices held, volunteer work, sports, travel, drama, art, music, etc.
- Indicate your level and intensity of interest in each activity (i.e., Grade 8 piano; played hockey for three years)
- Stress any achievements in the areas listed (i.e., came 1st in public speaking contest at school)

Unusual or unique interests can cause an employer to notice your resume above others. A discussion of them can provide a comfortable start to the job interview as well. For example, a potential employer, may talk about your hobbies or interest in sports to "break the ice" when you first begin your job interview.

THE THIRD STEP: YOUR REFERENCES

Your references can provide the credibility you need to get that special job. Don't assume your references won't be called. For most jobs, at least one of your references will be contacted. For more important jobs, all of them will be questioned about your abilities and personality.

You must be sure that your references will give you a positive recommendation for the jobs for which you are applying. For this reason, you should talk with them beforehand to let each of them know what you are doing and to find out if they support you in your endeavors. While they won't tell you what they are going to say, they might alleviate any concerns about providing you with a positive reference.

Here are some more points about your references:

- It's usual to state "supplied on request"
- Often your list of references is not needed until after the first interview
- They should be included if they are requested

When your references are requested they should include:

- The complete name and title of each person
- Their profession
- Their complete address
- Their telephone number

THE CHRONOLOGICAL RESUME: A TYPICAL BEGINNING

Let's now look at how our "typical" student, who is called Susan Q. Student, filled out the first draft of her chronological resume.

Shortly, we'll examine how to modify it to suit a specific job for which she is interested. If you haven't done so, make a copy of the sample resume worksheet at the end of the chapter and begin working on yours.

If this is your booklet, use the notes sections to make notes about things you need to remember to do or points that you think are especially important to you.

Now, examine Ms Student's resume, presented on the next page, in terms of the step-by-step approach to resume writing taken in this chapter.

THE STANDARD CHRONOLOGICAL RESUME: EXAMPLE OF A FIRST DRAFT

SUSAN Q. STUDENT
Common Address
Anytown, State/Province
Postal/Zip Code
(Area Code)-Telephone Number

EDUCATION:

1994	Graduation Diploma (B+ average); Pope Xavier High School -Courses in Social Sciences

WORK EXPERIENCE:

Summer '92 & '93	Office Assistant, Carpets R Us -Answered phones -Inputted data into computer
Summer '93	Salesperson, Arsenio's Fashions -Helped set up in-store displays -Advised customers about fashion co-ordination
Summer '92	Camp Counselor, Camp Minnewanka -Planned & supervised recreational activities
Other	Landscape Maintenance; Waitress

INTERESTS:

Volunteer	Phone Counselor at Distress Line
Sports	Playing Tennis; Coaching Soccer
Drama	Acted in High School Productions Coordinated Props

REFERENCES: Supplied on Request

RESUME WORKSHEET

Name:
Street Address:
Town, State/Province
Postal/Zip Code:
Telephone:

Objectives:

EDUCATION

Dates	Details

SKILLS

Type of Skill	Detail

RESUME WORKSHEET

WORK EXPERIENCE

Dates	Details

INTERESTS

Area	Details

RESUME WORKSHEET

REFERENCES

[Note: If your references are submitted separately from your resume, then make sure that your name, address and telephone number are at the top of your reference list.]

1. Name/Title of Reference:

Profession:
Address:

Telephone:

2. Name/Title of Reference:

Profession:
Address:

Telephone:

3. Name/Title of Reference:

Profession:
Address:

Telephone:

NOTES

Chapter Three

FINE-TUNING YOUR RESUME

TYPES OF RESUMES

Your resume is meant to be a tool to sell you to a potential employer. Since every person is different, it follows that every resume will be different. With this in mind, here are some more notes for you to read as you work towards producing the perfect resume for yourself. As you work through this material, look back at the sample resume that was given in Chapter Two (*The First Draft*) of this booklet.

Many books are available that provide hundreds of examples of resumes. Such examples can serve as useful guides but don't be fooled into simply replacing their information content with your own information. Since everyone is different, it is very unlikely that you will find a sample resume designed exactly to reflect your experience and accomplishments.

There's a good chance that by simply copying other resumes, you will miss some of your own personal strengths that could get you that important interview. You can also bet that your potential employer has seen all of these variants before. They are professionals and can easily tell an original resume from a store-bought copy. So, a fresh approach is often best. If you want to do well, you should decide for yourself what is best to include in your own resume.

Below is a summary of the basic types of resumes. In Chapter Two, we put together a basic chronological resume. In this chapter we will be looking at transforming Susan Q. Student's standard chronological resume into one that is more targeted for a specific job.

You should use the format that best suits your experience or the specific job for which you are applying.

BASIC TYPES OF RESUMES

A. STANDARD CHRONOLOGICAL (detailed in Chapter Two):

- Good for general applications (i.e., for any general summer or part-time job)
- Lists work experience, training, and schooling in strict chronological order
- Detailed in Chapter Two

B. MODIFIED CHRONOLOGICAL OR JOB -ORIENTED:

- Used when applying for a specific type of job
- Details the most relevant experience first
- Gives detailed information about experiences that relate to the job applied for
- It is selective: it downplays experience that isn't relevant to the job

C. VARIATIONS:

- The variations are endless
- Every resume is unique

- There is no single, correct way to prepare a resume
- There are many wrong ways to prepare a resume
- Design yours to best reflect your abilities

WRITING A MODIFIED CHRONOLOGICAL OR JOB-ORIENTED RESUME

Now it's time to transform the standard chronological resume into a job-oriented one. We'll do it in a step-by-step manner.

Rather than just listing work and related experience in strict chronological order, you can highlight relevant experience by grouping it together early in the resume.

In the example on page 21, note how the related volunteer and paid experience has been listed first. Note also how short descriptions of that experience highlight Susan's abilities which are relevant to her objective. Including an objective can impress the reader with how very focused you are.

EXAMPLE OF A JOB-ORIENTED RESUME
(E.g., summer job application)

SUSAN Q. STUDENT
Common Address
Anytown, State/Province
Postal/Zip Code
Telephone Number

OBJECTIVE(S): To provide supportive assistance to challenged children for the summer

EDUCATION:

1994 Graduation Diploma (B+ average); Pope Xavier High School; Courses in Social Sciences
Note: Plan to enroll in the Social Worker Certificate program at College

RELATED EXPERIENCE:

1993-94 Life Skills Support Worker, Community Living
Assisted with feeding & provided day-to-day life skills support to mentally challenged children

Summer 1992 Camp Counselor, Camp Minnewanka
Supervised up to 8 children 6-8 years of age
Planned & organized recreational activities
Provided a parental support system

1991-92 Phone Advisor Distress Line
Support to children in distress
Completed 6 Week Training Course

Page 1 of 2

Page 2

OTHER WORK EXPERIENCE:

Summer '92 & '93	**Office Assistant, Carpets R Us** Rectified customer complaints Inputted data to computer Answered phone & referred clients Managed a high volume of customer requests
Summer '93	**Salesperson, Arsenio's Fashions** Set up in-store displays Advised customers about fashion coordination Salesperson of the Month (twice)
Previous Experience	Landscape Maintenance Waitress

SKILLS:

Languages	Fluent in Written and Spoken French
Computers	Familiar with WordPerfect

INTERESTS:

Sports	Playing Baseball and Tennis Coaching Community Soccer for 3 years
Drama	Acted in two High School productions; coordinated props
REFERENCES	Supplied on Request

TIPS TO REMEMBER

When designing a standard chronological or a job-oriented resume, don't forget the items detailed on the following pages.

THE APPROACH

You Should Always:

- Be Concise and Factual
- Stress Achievements, Results and Challenges
- Stress Promotions
- Indicate Increases in Responsibility
- Avoid Unrelated, Personal Information
- Reminder: Be Positive

TECHNICAL DETAILS

Clean up your resume. It will never be perfect, but you can try.

You Should:

- Use Spacing Between Areas for Easy Reading
- Use Capitals, Bolding or Underlining to highlight key facts

- To make important details stand out and improve readability:

  —Avoid Long Lines of Type

  —Use Point Form or Narrative Style

  —Be Concise

- Have No Spelling or Grammatical Errors (It helps to have someone else read it for you.)

Remember: A sloppy, careless resume indicates a potentially sloppy and careless employee!

TALK TO SOMEONE WITH EXPERIENCE

Now that you're on track and have a resume that you feel is ready to present, you should get some input from others. The more experienced they are at preparing and/or evaluating resumes, the more useful their input will be.

For example you should see your school counselor or, get input from others who have worked in the same area as you are interested in. If this is not possible, any input is preferable to none.

In the next chapter, we'll give you a lot more helpful hints to improve your resume further. Then we'll move on to the cover letter.

Chapter four

LOADS OF HELPFUL HINTS

MORE HELPFUL HINTS

Along the way, we've already given you lots of useful hints about writing and fine-tuning your resume. At this point, a list of other valuable points is given for several different aspects of preparing your resume. You should look at each of them and apply them as you see fit.

STYLE

- ☐ Don't be too creative: Drawings on your resume are out; conservatism is in.

- ☐ Always be consistent with capitals, numbering, spacing throughout your resume.

- ☐ Avoid negative and irrelevant facts.

- ☐ Avoid long lines of writing across the page. Narrow columns are easier to read.

- ☐ Watch your grammar, style and appearance: Make your resume error free.

APPEARANCE

- ☐ Text-edit and laser print your resume (or, have it professionally done) for impressive results.

- ☐ It's best not to use a cover page for your resume. It just gets in the way and adds unnecessary bulk. It also looks amateurish.

- ☐ Use a high quality paper. Many companies produce special, resume paper that is appealing to the eye.

REFERENCES

- ☐ Always get permission from your references to use their names.

- ☐ Give a copy of your resume to each of your references: They can use this to refresh their memory if contacted.

- ☐ If you think it may help, let your references know when they may be contacted for an important job. Also, let them know a bit about the skill the employer is looking for.

- ☐ Keep your references on a separate sheet of the same type of paper as your resume. Then it can be included or submitted later preserving a quality image.

OTHER

- ☐ Don't miss that important phone call: Make sure an answering machine is on at the number given or have an alternative number where you can be reached or messages can be left.

- ☐ Your education consists of more than just schoolwork. Be sure to also list seminars, workshops and courses, if they specifically relate to the job in question.

☐ Keep a copy of your resume handy for revisions and updates.

☐ When there are some major new additions, don't forget to submit a new resume to companies that have your old one on file.

E. A LIST OF ACTION WORDS TO USE

Why not use some of these verbs in your resume and your cover letter if they apply:

achieved
analyzed
arranged
attained
budgeted
calculated
clarified
collected
compiled
convinced
coordinated
customized
designed
developed
diagnosed
directed
enabled
evaluated
examined
expanded
expedited
facilitated

forecasted
founded
generated
guided
implemented
improved
increased
influenced
initiated
instructed
introduced
managed
mediated
motivated
organized
overhauled
planned
produced
projected
recommended
recorded
scheduled
stimulated
supervised
tabulated
trained
translated
upgraded
wrote

Hint: Why not list some of your own action words here. Go through a thesaurus looking up each of the words listed above and add them to the list. We've left room for you to do this.

RESUME CHECKLIST

- ☐ Is your name, address and telephone number correct?
- ☐ Will the telephone number you gave always be answered?
- ☐ Have you clearly listed your objectives?
- ☐ Do your objectives meet the need of the specific job?
- ☐ Is your education section complete?
- ☐ Have you included all useful skills?
- ☐ Have you listed all other jobs you've held?
- ☐ Are your accomplishments stressed?
- ☐ Is all of your job-related experience included?

RESUME CHECKLIST
Continued

- ☐ Have you been positive throughout?
- ☐ Is it 1 or 2 pages at most?
- ☐ Is it completely honest?
- ☐ Have you written it using commonly used words?
- ☐ Have you avoided trite or overly used phrases?
- ☐ Have you avoided irrelevant technical details?
- ☐ Have you prepared/included an accurate list of references?
- ☐ Have you contacted your references?

It's always a good idea to see what has worked for others. For example, you could review a variety of resume books in local and school libraries to get ideas for other types that might suit your style. Remember the earlier warning about copying these sample resumes. It would also be wise for you to visit an employment counselor to get feedback on your approach.

Chapter Five

THE COVER LETTER

THE CONTENTS OF THE COVER LETTER

Within certain limits, the cover letter should be set up in a certain way. It should also address specific points. After that the cover letter is up to you and should be modified as appropriate to the job for which you are applying. So, let's look at the construction of a typical cover letter and its contents. Then we'll look at a sample letter.

HOW TO SET UP A COVER LETTER

Your Street address
Apt/Unit #
City/Town, Province/State
Postal/Zip Code
Telephone #

Date

Name of Hiring Person
Title/Position
Company Name
Address
City, State/Province
Zip/Postal Code

Dear Mr., Mrs., Ms., Dr., Prof. (Person's Surname):

FIRST PARAGRAPH

- Indicate why you are writing
- State job or type of employment you are applying for
- Tell how you heard of job opening

MIDDLE PARAGRAPHS

- Show how you fit the job description
- Summarize & interpret resume as it applies to the position
- Sell personal attributes that will help you get hired
- Explain why you want the specific job

CLOSING PARAGRAPH

- Mention that your resume is enclosed
- Indicate that you will be in touch with them within a set time frame to discuss the possibility of an interview.
- Encourage them to respond

Yours truly,

I. M. Keen

Encl.

Susan Q. Student
Common Address
Anytown, State/Province
Postal/Zip Code
(555) 555-5555

January 27, 1994

Mrs. R. Clement, Case Manager
Oakland Center
1206 Byers Street
Grover, State/Province
Postal/Zip Code

Dear Mrs. Clement,

Your advertisement for a summer support worker in the January 26th issue of 'Opportunities' magazine caught my attention. My volunteer and paid work experience with children, particularly the mentally challenged, provide me with the skills that the job description outlines.

My volunteer experience as a life support worker with Community Living parallels the job you describe. The phone advisor position with Distress Line and the camp counseling experience at Camp Minnewanka have further developed my helping and listening skills. I always enjoyed the social sciences in school and plan to enroll part-time in the social worker certificate program at my local college.

I have been impressed with the articles that I've read in the Daily Gazette outlining the community outreach programs that the Oaklands Center has initiated. I am enthusiastic about being part of such a creative organization.

I look forward to discussing my qualifications with you further at an interview.

Sincerely,

Susan Q. Student

Encl.

Note: Our sample letter is spread over two pages due to the size limitations of these published pages. A proper cover letter is only one page in length.

THE COVER LETTER: THINGS TO DO

- ☐ Show how you fit *all* of the requirements as outlined in the job description. Use factual examples. Interpret the resume for your employer.

- ☐ Make sure all words are spelled correctly.

- ☐ Be sure the name and position of the contact person is correct.

- ☐ Be assertive but don't use the pronoun "I" too often.

- ☐ Make sure the content of your letter is organized.

- ☐ Give a telephone number that will be answered.

- ☐ Where expertise is lacking, indicate personal qualities, innate abilities and a willingness to learn.

- ☐ Be succinct: Keep your letter to one page!

- ☐ Every cover letter should be original. Don't use a photocopy or form letter with details inserted.

- ☐ Don't forget to sign your letter.

- ☐ Use the same kind of paper as used for your resume.

- ☐ Focus on the employer's needs, not your own.

- ☐ Use simple and precise language. Avoid timeworn and other empty phrases.

- ☐ Incorporate your own creative style. Don't copy redundant examples.

- ☐ Use "action" words to make your letter more dynamic.

- ☐ Remember: Let the employer know what you can do for them. Be clear about how your knowledge and abilities relate to their needs.

NOTES

Basic Concepts LEARNING GUIDES©

TITLES TO CHOOSE FROM:

How to Write Tests & Exams
ISBN 1-895482-11-9
How to Study & Learn
ISBN 1-895482-12-7
How to Write Excellent Notes
ISBN 1-895482-13-5
How to Write Reports & Essays
ISBN 1-895482-14-3
How to Get Things Done!
ISBN 1-895482-15-1
How to Give a Classroom Talk
ISBN 1-895482-16-X
How to Write a Resume & Cover Letter
ISBN 1-895482-17-8

✱Special *Step-by-Step* Techniques✱

✱Methods that Work✱

✱Lots of Helpful Hints✱

✱Easy to Read✱

More titles under development

48pp; wire stitch; $3.95 USA; $4.95 Canada

TRILOBYTE PRESS

HOW TO SUCCEED AT COLLEGE Second Edition

Danton H. O'Day, Ph.D.

ISBN 1-895482-09-7
180pp; ©1993

Deals with everything college students need to know to survive and succeed. Everything that a student needs for success is addressed in clear cut language.

Here's what students say about Prof. O'Day's books:
"I was inspired. Thanks for your priceless advice."
"Your book helped me realize I could do it."
"Excellent!"

HOW TO SUCCEED AT UNIVERSITY

Danton H. O'Day, Ph.D.

ISBN 0-921627-19-X
186pp; ©1990

The Canadian bestseller!

No academic stone is left unturned in this down to earth, honest account of life at university. As a result of the success of his books, professor O'Day was **commissioned by the Canadian government** to write a survival guide for Canada Scholarship students entitled The Savvy Scholar: How to retain your Canada scholarship.

STUDENT TIME MANAGER

Nora J. Lewis, Ph.D.

The *first* self-help book on planning and time management written for students. Addresses all of the common problems students have with getting organized and setting priorities. Provides basic methods to help overcome them.

***Everything* students need to know for:**

- Meeting Deadlines
- Taking Control of Their Lives
- Getting Better Grades
- Gaining Self-Confidence
- Preparing for a Successful Future

Includes:

Proven Problem Solving Techniques
New Approaches
Helpful Advice

All the Power Techniques used by professionals written for the student. The skills learned from this book will pay immediate dividends and will continue to reward as long as they are used.

ISBN 1-895482-04-6
140 pp; $12.95 USA; $14.95Canada
Illustrated

ORDER INFORMATION

Use the following form (plus check or money order)
or, send a purchase order to:

Canada:
TRILOBYTE PRESS
1486 Willowdown Road
Oakville, ON L6L 1X3

USA:
TRILOBYTE PRESS
Unit 443, 825 E Roosevelt Rd
Lombard, IL 60148

Or, **FAX** Your Order:

(416) 847-3258

(708) 916-1148

Quantity	**Item**	**Cost**
	How to Succeed at College ($12.95 US; $14.95 Canada)	
	How to Succeed at University ($11.95 Canada only)	
	Student Time Manager ($12.95 US; $14.95 Canada)	
	Basic Concepts Learning Guides© ($3.95 US; $4.95 Canada each) How to Study & Learn How to Write Tests & Exams How to Write Reports & Essays How to Give a Classroom Talk How to Plan & Get Organized How to Write Resumes & Cover Letters How to Find That Job	
Subtotal		
Shipping & Handling ($3.00 or 5%, whichever is greater)		
GST (add 7%; Canada only)		
TOTAL AMOUNT DUE		